GOD'S MESSY
FAMILY

FINDING YOUR PLACE WHEN LIFE ISN'T PERFECT

**Leader Guide
by Martha
Bettis Gee**

JACOB ARMSTRONG

Abingdon Press
Nashville

GOD'S MESSY FAMILY
FINDING YOUR PLACE WHEN LIFE ISN'T PERFECT
Leader Guide

Copyright © 2018 Abingdon Press
All rights reserved.

ISBN 978-1-5018-4358-7

18 19 20 21 22 23 24 25 26 27—10 9 8 7 6 5 4 3 2 1
MANUFACTURED IN THE UNITED STATES OF AMERICA

CONTENTS

To the Leader. 5

1. The Myth of the Perfect Family. 10

2. The Gap Between What God Says and What You See. 19

3. No, Nothing Is Too Hard for the Lord 28

4. Loss and Promise in the Family of God. 37

5. Promise Maker and Promise Keeper 46

6. The Beauty of Imperfection. 56

God's Messy Family

Finding Your Place When Life Isn't Perfect

God's Messy Family
978-1-5018-4356-3
978-1-5018-4357-0 eBook

God's Messy Family: Leader Guide
978-1-5018-4358-7
978-1-5018-4359-4 eBook

God's Messy Family: DVD
978-1-5018-4360-0

The Connected Life:
Small Groups That Create Community

This handy and helpful guide describes how churches can set up, maintain, and nurture small groups to create a congregation that is welcoming and outward-looking. Written by founding pastor Jacob Armstrong with Rachel Armstrong, the guide is based on the pioneering small group ministry of Providence United Methodist Church in Mt. Juliet, Tennessee.

978-1-5018-4345-7
978-1-5018-4346-4 eBook

Also by Jacob Armstrong:
A New Playlist: Hearing Jesus in a Noisy World (The Connected Life Series)
Interruptions: A 40-Day Journey with Jesus
Loving Large
Renovate: Building a Life with God (The Connected Life Series)
The God Story
Treasure: A Four-Week Study on Faith and Money
Upside Down

With Jorge Acevedo:
Sent: Delivering the Gift of Hope at Christmas

With James W. Moore:
Christmas Gifts That Won't Break: Expanded Edition with Devotions

With Adam Hamilton and Mike Slaughter:
The New Adapters

TO THE LEADER

Welcome! In this study, you have the opportunity to help a group of learners explore the family of God. The study is based on Jacob Armstrong's book, *God's Messy Family: Finding Your Place When Life Isn't Perfect.*

Jacob Armstrong is founding pastor of Providence Church, a United Methodist congregation in Mt. Juliet, Tennessee. Armstrong addresses his book to those of us for whom life often feels messy, imperfect, and dysfunctional. Despite the mess of our daily lives, he recognizes that most of us still want to be included and connected. Even the most broken and imperfect people can find a place of belonging and meaning in God's messy family. Despite our many imperfections, despite our brokenness, each of us can find a seat at the table of God's family.

Through an exploration of our spiritual connection to the family of Abraham and Sarah, we come face to face with the affirmation that God's family is our family. And as members of the family, all the promises, miracles, and healing are ours to claim.

Scripture tells us that where two or three are gathered together, we can be assured of the presence of the Holy Spirit, working in and through all those gathered. As you prepare to lead, pray for that presence and expect that you will experience it.

The study includes six sessions, and it makes use of the following components:

- *God's Messy Family: Finding Your Place When Life Isn't Perfect*, by Jacob Armstrong;
- the DVD that accompanies the study;
- this Leader Guide.

Participants in the study will also need Bibles, as well as either a spiral-bound notebook for a journal or an electronic means of journaling, such as a tablet. If possible, notify those interested in the study in advance of the first session. Make arrangements for them to get copies of the book so that they can read the introduction and chapter 1 before the first group meeting.

Using This Guide with Your Group

Because no two groups are alike, this guide has been designed to give you flexibility and choice in tailoring the sessions for your group. The session format is listed below. You may choose any or all of the activities, adapting them as you wish to meet the schedule and needs of your particular group.

The leader guide offers a basic session plan designed to be completed in a session of about 45 minutes in length. Select ahead of time which activities the group will do, for how long, and in what order. Depending on which activities you select, there may be special preparation needed. The leader is alerted in the session plan when advance preparation is needed.

Session Format

Planning the Session

Session Goals
Scriptural Foundation
Special Preparation

Getting Started

> Opening Activity
> Opening Prayer

Learning Together

> Video Study and Discussion
> Book and Bible Study and Discussion
> More Activities (Optional)

Wrapping Up

> Closing Activity
> Closing Prayer

Helpful Hints

Preparing for the Session

- Pray for the leading of the Holy Spirit as you prepare for the study. Pray for discernment for yourself and for each member of the study group.
- Before each session, familiarize yourself with the content. Read the book chapter again.
- Choose the session elements you will use during the group session, including the specific discussion questions you plan to cover. Be prepared, however, to adjust the session as group members interact and as questions arise. Prepare carefully, but allow space for the Holy Spirit to move in and through the group members and through you as facilitator.
- Prepare the room where the group will meet so that the space will enhance the learning process. Ideally, group members should be seated around a table or in a circle so that all can see each other. Moveable chairs are best because the group will often be forming pairs or small groups for discussion.

- Bring a supply of Bibles for those who forget to bring their own. Also bring writing paper and pens for those participants who do not bring a journal or a tablet or other electronic means of journaling.
- For most sessions you will also need a chalkboard and chalk, a whiteboard and markers, or an easel with large sheets of paper and markers.

Shaping the Learning Environment

- Begin and end on time.
- Create a climate of openness, encouraging group members to participate as they feel comfortable.
- Remember that some people will jump right in with answers and comments, while others need time to process what is being discussed.
- If you notice that some group members seem never to be able to enter the conversation, ask them if they have thoughts to share. Give everyone a chance to talk, but keep the conversation moving. Moderate to prevent a few individuals from doing all the talking.
- Communicate the importance of group discussions and group exercises.
- If no one answers at first during discussions, do not be afraid of silence. Count silently to ten, then say something such as, "Would anyone like to go first?" If no one responds, venture an answer yourself and ask for comments.
- Model openness as you share with the group. Group members will follow your example. If you limit your sharing to a surface level, others will follow suit.
- Encourage multiple answers or responses before moving on.
- To help continue a discussion and give it greater depth, ask, "Why?" or "Why do you believe that?" or "Can you say more about that?"

- Affirm others' responses with comments such as "Great" or "Thanks" or "Good insight," especially if it's the first time someone has spoken during the group session.
- Monitor your own contributions. If you are doing most of the talking, back off so that you do not train the group to listen rather than speak up.
- Remember that you do not have all the answers. Your job is to keep the discussion going and encourage participation.

Managing the Session

- Honor the time schedule. If a session is running longer than expected, get consensus from the group before continuing beyond the agreed-upon ending time.
- Involve group members in various aspects of the group session, such as saying prayers or reading the Scripture.
- Note that the session guides sometimes call for breaking into smaller groups or pairs. This gives everyone a chance to speak and participate fully. Mix up the groups; don't let the same people pair up for every activity.
- As always in discussions that may involve personal sharing, confidentiality is essential. Group members should never pass along stories that have been shared in the group. Remind the group members at each session: confidentiality is crucial to the success of this study.

1

THE MYTH OF
THE PERFECT FAMILY

Planning the Session

Session Goals

As a result of conversations and activities connected with this session, group members should begin to

- explore, through the story of Abram and Sarai, what Scripture reveals about God's messy family;
- examine the myth of the perfect family;
- reflect on the implications of being a blessing to the whole world.

Scriptural Foundation

> *The Lord had said to Abram, "Go from your country, your people and your father's household to the land I will show you.*

"I will make you into a great nation,
    and I will bless you;
I will make your name great,
    and you will be a blessing.
I will bless those who bless you,
    and whoever curses you I will curse;
and all peoples on earth
    will be blessed through you."

(Genesis 12:1-3)

Special Preparation

- If participants are not familiar with one another, provide nametags.
- Have available a notebook or paper and a pen or pencil for anyone who did not bring a notebook or an electronic device for journaling.
- Print the following on separate sheets of paper and post at intervals around your space: *Leave It to Beaver, All in the Family, The Jeffersons, Roseanne, Parenthood, Modern Family.*
- If you are not familiar with the series *This Is Us*, it would be helpful to view one or more episodes prior to the study. You can view episodes from Season 1 and Season 2 at www.NBC.com.
- Decide if you will use either of the optional additional activities. If you will be creating altars, you will need tape and felt-tipped markers. Also prepare "rocks" by cutting sheets of printer paper or construction paper into rough ovals—enough for each participant to have at least two. Set aside wall or board space in two locations for taping up the rocks to make the altars.
- Decide if you will use the hymn "The God of Abraham Praise" or another hymn of praise. Obtain the lyrics and, if needed, arrange for accompaniment.

Getting Started

Opening Activity

As participants arrive, welcome them to the study. Invite them to move around the room reading the titles of past TV series that focused on the family. When most have arrived, gather together. Ask them to respond to the following:

- My name is _____, and a TV series about the family that I remember is _____.

When everyone has had a chance to respond, invite volunteers to describe how the family was portrayed in one of the series they remember, either one of the posted titles or another series they enjoyed. Then ask:

- How does your own experience of family life compare with what you saw portrayed in that series?

Call the group's attention to the book's introduction. If participants have not had a chance to read it, invite them to scan the text quickly. Ask participants to indicate with a show of hands if they have watched the series *This Is Us*. Invite a volunteer to briefly summarize how the author, Jacob Armstrong, characterizes the series.

Point out that Armstrong uses the example of TV series about families as the starting point for considering our own families. In this study, participants will be exploring their place in what Armstrong calls God's messy family. They will encounter how all of us are included at the table and connected to others in God's family, regardless of our imperfections.

Opening Prayer

Pray the following prayer, or one of your own choosing:

Gracious God, each of us comes to this place bringing our unique experiences of messy, unpredictable family life. Guide us as we seek to better understand your messy family. By your Spirit, give us a sense of your boundless hospitality. Open our hearts to your invitation to take our place at your table, regardless of our flaws and imperfections. Amen.

Learning Together

Video Study and Discussion

In this first chapter of the study, the author, Jacob Armstrong, introduces us to the idea that, like our own families, the family of Abram and Sarai was flawed and at times dysfunctional. The story of this family draws us in to an understanding of our own place in the messy family of God—a family to which all of us belong. Armstrong, founding pastor of Providence Church, a United Methodist congregation in Mt. Juliet, Tennessee, gives us an overview of the story of Abram and Sarai's family, a family that shatters the myth of the perfect family. After viewing the video segment, discuss some of the following:

- In what ways does Jacob Armstrong's review of the scriptural story of Abram's family jibe with what you remember about that family's story? Were there details or episodes Armstrong mentioned that you found surprising or that you were unaware of? If so, which ones? Where do you see evidence that Abram's family was messy and flawed?
- Armstrong relates some anecdotes about experiences he has had with family meals. Which stories resonate for you? Can you name similar experiences around your own family table, either positive or negative?
- What would it be like if we lived into the family to which we belong? What would you say is the difference between being part of a perfect family and walking toward perfection together?

Book and Bible Study and Discussion

Examine the Myth of the Perfect Family

To explore more deeply what Armstrong calls the myth of the perfect family, invite participants to form pairs and respond to the following:

- How would you describe the perfect family?

After allowing a few minutes for pairs to discuss, ask each pair to give one defining characteristic they identified, and make a list of these characteristics on a large sheet of paper or a board.

Remind the group that there are many ways to describe one's family. For some it may be their nuclear biological family, for others it may be an extended family, and for still others it may be people unrelated to them by blood who nevertheless constitute a family. Discuss:

- How closely does our description of a perfect family match the makeup of your family? How closely does this description fit the picture of how you experience family life?
- Jacob Armstrong asserts that perfection is not the goal of family. What does he suggest is? How do you respond?

Explore the Story of Abram and Sarai's Family

Ask participants to quickly review what the chapter has to say about Abram's family, as well as recalling what Armstrong tells us in the video. Then ask a volunteer to read aloud Genesis 12:1-9, the passage that includes this session's foundational Scripture. Discuss the following:

- According to the Scripture, God's family had its beginning with Abram, Sarai, and Lot. In the light of what the scriptural story tells us, what is ironic about the names of Abram and Sarai?

We read that a more literal translation of God's command to "Go" is to "Walk." Invite participants to imagine such a command. Ask them to think about their own situation—their age, general health and fitness, and so forth. Ask:

- What would be particular challenges for you if you had to undertake such a journey?
- What obstacles might be the most daunting?

Assign to half the participants Genesis 12:10-20 and to the other half Genesis 13:1-17. Ask them to read their assigned passage silently and to review what the chapter tells us about the two accounts. Discuss:

- In what ways do these stories reveal that Abram and Sarai are typical, like us, with personal failings and foibles?
- Where in the story thus far can you see evidence of their greatness?

Invite group members to ponder in silence what in their own lives they might identify as signs of greatness—indications that they say yes to God and seek to walk with God. What weaknesses and failings can they pinpoint? Encourage them to jot these insights down in their journals.

Reflect on the Implications of Being a Blessing

Armstrong poses the question: How does God's family become a blessing? Distribute drawing paper and crayons or markers. Invite participants to imagine themselves on a journey of faith, walking toward the land where God will use their lives to bless others.

Ask them to choose a name they think exemplifies the person they are and have been—something that describes their normality, with all its shortcomings and flaws. They might want to use their present name coupled with a modifier—for instance, Norman the Nitpicker— or perhaps something like She Who Refuses to Admit When She Is Wrong.

Ask them to sketch a pathway that meanders from the left side of the paper to the right. Along the way, ask them to list those shortcomings and mistakes that have served as a barrier to saying yes to God and seeking to walk alongside God, as well as any notable occasions when their actions and attitudes have exemplified a blessing. Ask that they spend some moments reflecting on this pathway. Then invite them, at the far right of the paper, to choose a name that represents all they are seeking, in walking more closely with God and living into their names.

Point out that Armstrong discusses altars of praise and prayer. Ask participants to review what he has to say about these altars in the text. Then ask them to consider the following:

- When in my daily life do I pause to say thank you to God, remembering God's enduring presence and trustworthy love? How can I set aside a time and place for an altar of praise?
- When in my daily routine do I pause to call on the Lord? How can I set aside a time and place for an altar of prayer?

Encourage participants to jot down these questions in their journals and to continue considering them and taking action, in order to ensure that praise and prayer are regular practices.

More Activities (Optional)

Create Altars of Praise and Prayer

Invite participants to create altars of praise and prayer in your learning space, perhaps on opposite sides or in the corners. Label each space chosen, and give each person several of the paper "rocks" you prepared, as well as felt-tipped markers. Ask them to review what Armstrong tells us about each altar Abram created.

Ask group members to reflect on events or situations from the past week for which they would like to praise God, and have them jot down a phrase or sentence on a rock describing that event or situation. Invite them to tape their rock to the wall along with others to form an altar shape. Ask them to do the same for the altar of prayer, jotting down something about which they have called upon the name of the Lord in prayer (or something they plan to lift up in prayer).

Encourage them in the coming week to continue identifying situations to bring before God in prayer, either in supplication or in praise.

Role-Play Characters

Assign to half the participants Genesis 12:10-20 and to the other half Genesis 13:1-17. Randomly assign the following roles to participants in each of the two groups: in group 1 (12:10-20), assign each person either the role of Abram or the role of Sarai; in group 2 (13:1-17), assign people either Abram or Lot. Have each group read the assigned passage; then ask them to respond to the incident from the perspective of their assigned role. After allowing a few minutes, reconvene the large group to discuss the following:

- How would you describe the actions of each character: as representing human foibles or as expressing greatness? Why?
- How do you think Pharaoh would have described the family of Abram and Sarai?
- Why do you think Abram wanted to separate himself from Lot?

Wrapping Up

Invite participants to recall and briefly describe the stories of Armstrong's family around the table that he tells in both the chapter and the video segment. Invite volunteers to respond to the following:

- The story about family meals that I resonate most with is _____ because_____.

As an example of what it means to be welcomed at the table of God's family, encourage participants to reflect on how meals happen in their family. Suggest the following as points of reflection:

- If family members are together for a meal at some time during the week, suggest that group members take at least a little time to focus silently on each family member, seeking to truly hear and see him or her.

- If mealtime is chaotic or if family members do not eat together, ask participants to offer a simple silent prayer for each person.
- If a participant eats meals alone most of the time, suggest that before they begin to eat, they take a moment of silence to hold up before God in prayer each person they consider family.

Closing Activity

Remind the group that Abram built an altar of praise to God. Sing or recite together "The God of Abraham Praise" or another hymn of praise to God.

Remind the group to read chapter 2 before the next session.

Closing Prayer

Pray the following, or a prayer of your choosing:

Amazing God, we are so grateful that you have invited us to be a part of your family! Just as you told Abram and Sarai that their names would be great and all people on earth would be blessed through them, help us to live into our names. By your Spirit, lead us on this journey to be a blessing to others. Amen.

2

THE GAP BETWEEN WHAT GOD SAYS AND WHAT YOU SEE

Planning the Session

Session Goals

As a result of conversations and activities connected with this session, group members should begin to

- explore further, through the story of Abram and Sarai, what Scripture reveals about God's messy family;
- examine the gap time between the promise being made and the promise being fulfilled;
- reflect on the invitation to step outside of time and see what God is working on.

Scriptural Foundation

> *Abram said, "Sovereign Lord, what can you give me*
> *since I remain childless and the one who will inherit*

*my estate is Eliezer of Damascus?" And Abram said,
"You have given me no children; so a servant in my
household will be my heir."*

*[God] took him outside and said, "Look up at the sky
and count the stars—if indeed you can count them."
Then he said to him, "So shall your offspring be."*

*As the sun was setting, Abram fell into a deep sleep,
and a thick and dreadful darkness came over him.*

(Genesis 15:2-3, 5, 12)

Special Preparation

- You will need printing or drawing paper and felt-tipped markers for the opening activity.
- Have available a notebook or paper and a pen or pencil for anyone who did not bring a notebook or an electronic device for journaling.
- Decide if you will use either of the optional additional activities.
- If you decide to sing or recite "O God, Our Help in Ages Past" as a closing hymn, obtain hymnals with the hymn and, if needed, arrange for accompaniment.

Getting Started

Opening Activity

As participants arrive, welcome them. Invite those present for the first session to briefly explain about altars of praise and prayer and to what extent group members were successful in setting aside time during the past week for prayer and praise.

Gather together. Call the group's attention to what the author of the study tells us about the practice of taking a picture of one's child on the first day of the school year and posting it on social media, as well as his neighbor's sarcastic riff on that practice. Ask:

- What is the gap in your life that you are just waiting out?

Distribute paper and felt-tipped markers, and invite participants to make a sign indicating the gap they might display in a candid shot to be posted on Facebook or Instagram. It might be the number of days until retirement, or the length of time until a child completes college, or some shorter span such as the days until a much-anticipated vacation.

After allowing a few minutes for the group to work, invite volunteers to display their signs and add any explanation about what gap the sign represents. Ask:

- Why do you suppose it is difficult to live in the gap between where you are presently and where you would like to be?

You may want to take a snapshot of each person with their sign and print out the photos before the next session.

Opening Prayer

Pray the following prayer, or one of your own choosing:

Eternal God, we confess that sometimes we are so focused on where we want to go and what we want to be that we fail to appreciate the place where we are right now. Bring us into a quiet time in which, together, we can simply be—resting in the presence of your love. Guide us as we seek more clarity about your purpose for our lives. Amen.

Learning Together

Video Study and Discussion

In chapter 2, Jacob Armstrong introduces us to the idea that there can be a gap between what God promises and what a person is experiencing. He explores the realities and feelings people often experience in the meantime, as well as how God may be working in and through those gap times. After viewing the video segment, discuss some of the following:

- Jacob Armstrong describes a job he had as a young person in which his employer required him to sweep the floor during the gap times in the work. What was the purpose of the sweeping? What does he say about what he learned about who he was when he was sweeping?
- He observes that "the meantime" is most of the time, and most of the time we are sweeping. What does he mean? Has this been your experience? Why or why not?
- Armstrong speaks about aspects of who he is that were passed down from his parents. What aspects of yourself can you name that are part of your family heritage, passed down from your parents or grandparents?
- Armstrong notes that our spiritual heritage through Father Abraham is belief. How do you respond?

Book and Bible Study and Discussion

Explore the Story of Abram and Sarai

As a way of reviewing, and to bring new participants up to speed, invite volunteers to summarize briefly the following stories: Abram and Sarai's journey and God's promise in Genesis 12:1-9; Abram and Sarai in Egypt in verses 10-20; and Abram and Lot's parting ways in Genesis 13.

Then invite one or more volunteers to read aloud Genesis 15:1-6, 12. Discuss the following:

- Jacob Armstrong tells us that the story of Abram and Sarai is the biblical equivalent of the TV series *This Is Us*. What does he say about the importance of the gap in the narrative of the story of that show? What might be the importance of exploring the incidents in Abram's and Sarai's story between the time of God's promise and the time when it was brought to fruition?

Invite someone to read aloud Armstrong's paraphrase of Abram's plaintive complaint to God (beginning after the text says, "It's as if Abram was saying . . ."). Discuss:

- What was God's response to Abram's complaint?
- How did Abram respond to God?

Examine the Gap Time

Invite the group to respond to the following:

- How does Jacob Armstrong describe the gap that may exist between what we see and what God promises?
- What examples does he give from the story of Abram and Sarai to expand on how such a gap may be dark? long? messy?

We read that in living into and through gap times in our lives, patience is required. Discuss:

- Jacob Armstrong gives us the example of his impatience while waiting in the express line at the grocery store, and how even that experience has drastically changed with the advent of online ordering and picking up of groceries. What situations of waiting in your life give rise to your greatest impatience? Do they come as you wait in traffic? in dealing with slow computer functioning or Internet connections? in some other situation? What is usually your response in situations such as this?

We read in the chapter that one thing we learn from the story of Abram and Sarai is that God is very, very patient. Form two smaller groups and assign one of the following ideas to each group:

- God looks at timing differently than we do.
- God's seeming delays are all about keeping promises.

Ask each of the smaller groups to read over what the chapter has to say about their assigned statement. Ask them to then consider in what ways they affirm that statement, and what questions surface for them when they reflect on it.

After allowing a few minutes for the two groups to work, gather together as the large group and give each group the opportunity to report. Discuss any questions that have surfaced in the small group work and others that come up as the total group discusses.

Reflect on the Gap

Remind participants of the story Armstrong relates of his first job at the feed store, and what he learned from his "in the meantime" task of sweeping the store. Then ask participants to reflect on the following and to respond in writing to one or more in their journals. They may want to head this entry, "In the meantime."

- Am I presently engaged in the equivalent of the more exciting aspects of my spiritual life, or am I "in the meantime"?
- If I feel my life is in "gap time," am I facing a mess? experiencing a dark period? gripped by impatience? Can I nevertheless sense that God is working, or do I have no sense of that?
- If I am experiencing a gap or a mess, have I, like Abram and Sarai, attempted to take matters into my own hands? In what ways?
- What spiritual tools are available to me to help me live into the gap and step out of time?

Encourage participants in the coming week to bring into sharper focus the "sweeping" aspects of their daily lives—those seemingly mundane tasks at home, at school, or in the workplace that take up the majority of their time. As a spiritual discipline, invite them to try to pause briefly in the midst of those tasks to bring into awareness a sense of God working in and through them.

More Activities (Optional)

Explore a Spiritual Gap Year

Call the group's attention to the practice of some young people when they graduate from high school of taking what is called a "gap year." Discuss:

- What is the idea behind taking a gap year? What kinds of experiences do young people typically seek during the gap year? Ideally, what will a young person gain from this practice?

Invite participants to imagine they are going to take a spiritual gap year—a time in which they might assess their spiritual lives. Form pairs, and ask each pair to discuss the following:

- If I took a spiritual gap year, what might I refrain from doing? What things might I begin to do?
- What spiritual practices might help me assess my life of faith? What might help me be more aware of God's presence in and through the ordinary events of my daily life? What might help me be more aware of God working in and through those seemingly insignificant events?

After allowing time for pairs to work, gather together in the large group. In turn, ask each pair to report one thing they discussed, and jot those ideas down on a large sheet of paper. Continue until the group has exhausted their ideas. Encourage participants to consider incorporating at least one suggested idea or practice into their own daily life.

Explore Another Story of Abraham and Sarah

Armstrong refers to the story of Ishmael's birth. If participants are less than familiar with the scriptural account, invite them to explore this story. Ask one or more volunteers to read aloud both Genesis 16 and Genesis 21:8-21. Discuss some of the following:

- What does this story reveal about the extent of the patience of Abraham and Sarah in waiting for God's promise to be fulfilled?
- What is messy about the way that Sarah reacted? about how Abraham acquiesced to Sarah's response?
- Who was harmed by the impatience of Abraham and Sarah?

Wrapping Up

Invite the group to listen in silence as you read the following verses from Romans 4 aloud.

"Abraham believed God, and it was credited to him as righteousness."

It was not through the law that Abraham and his offspring received the promise that he would be heir of the world, but through the righteousness that comes by faith.

Therefore, the promise comes by faith, so that it may be by grace and may be guaranteed to all Abraham's offspring—not only to those who are of the law but also to those who have the faith of Abraham. He is the father of us all.

Without weakening in his faith, he faced the fact that his body was as good as dead—since he was about a hundred years old—and that Sarah's womb was also dead. Yet he did not waver through unbelief regarding the promise of God, but was strengthened in his faith and gave glory to God, being fully persuaded that God had power to do what he had promised.

(Romans 4:3, 13, 16, 19-21)

Invite participants to think about the situations in which they presently find themselves, and reflect on the following:

- Do you think your life, however messy or dark or merely mundane it may be, compares in unlikelihood to the situation of a hundred-year-old man and his equally elderly wife being the parents of offspring as numerous as the stars? If so, in what ways?
- How do you respond to the idea that you are exactly where God wants you to be? Is that a source of comfort and hope? Or are you skeptical, discouraged, or despairing? Why?

Allow time for any comments, questions, or observations participants may want to express.

Remind the group to read chapter 3 before the next session.

Closing Activity

Point out that in 2 Peter 3:8, we read:

> *Do not forget this one thing, dear friends: With the Lord a day is like a thousand years, and a thousand years are like a day.*

Invite the group to sing or recite together "O God, Our Help in Ages Past."

Closing Prayer

Pray the following, or a prayer of your choosing:

Loving God, we want to believe! In the midst of our sometimes messy, often mundane lives, we yearn to hear your voice saying, "I can't wait to fulfill these great promises in you." Make us ever more aware of your presence in these in-between times, and give us patience and clarity. Amen.

3

NO, NOTHING IS TOO HARD FOR THE LORD

Planning the Session

Session Goals

As a result of conversations and activities connected with this session, group members should begin to

- explore further, through the story of Abraham and Sarah, what Scripture reveals about God's messy family;
- examine radical hospitality;
- reflect on seeing stars in midday.

Scriptural Foundation

Then the Lord said to Abraham, "Why did Sarah laugh and say, 'Will I really have a child, now that I am old?' Is anything too hard for the Lord? I will

return to you at the appointed time next year, and
Sarah will have a son."

(Genesis 18:13-14)

Now the Lord was gracious to Sarah as he had said,
and the Lord did for Sarah what he had promised.
Sarah became pregnant and bore a son to Abraham
in his old age, at the very time God had promised
him. Abraham gave the name Isaac [which means He
Laughs] *to the son Sarah bore him.*

(Genesis 21:1-3)

Special Preparation

- Continue to make available materials for journaling to anyone who did not bring a journal.
- To prepare for exploring the Scriptures, practice reading aloud Genesis 18:1-15 and Genesis 21:1-7.
- For the reflecting activity, you will need drawing paper and felt-tipped markers.
- Decide if you will use either of the optional additional activities. For the additional activity on hospitality, print the following on a large sheet of paper:
  - ◊ How might I more intentionally acknowledge the humanity of this person?
  - ◊ How might it be possible to act in more hospitable ways in my interactions with this person?
- For the closing activity, choose a song of joy to sing or recite together. Three possibilities are "I've Got Peace Like a River," "I've Got the Joy, Joy, Joy, Joy Down in My Heart," or "You Shall Go Out with Joy." Get the lyrics and, if needed, arrange for accompaniment.

Getting Started

Opening Activity

As participants arrive, welcome them. Gather together. If you printed out pictures of participants that you took in the opening activity, display those and invite comments about the gaps that participants were demonstrating. Invite volunteers to report on their experiences in the past week of attempting to bring into sharper focus the "sweeping" aspects of their daily lives—tasks at home, at school, or in the workplace that take up the majority of their time. How successful were they in pausing in the midst of those tasks to bring into awareness a sense of God working in and through them? Encourage them to continue this spiritual practice. Ask:

- How do you feel about the name your parents chose for you? Do you like it? Do you think it is a good fit for the person you are?
- If you are not particularly fond of your name, what would you change your name to? Why?
- Do you think your name can have any impact on how others perceive you or on how you perceive yourself? If so, how?

Ask those who know the meaning of their name to report to the group. Others with smartphones may want to do a search to discover what their name means and also to check for the meaning of a name they would prefer to have.

Remind those who were present for session 1 about the activity in which they were asked to choose a name they thought exemplified the person they are and have been—something that describes their normality, with all its shortcomings and flaws, perhaps their present name coupled with a modifier. Then they were invited to choose a name that represents all they are seeking to be in walking more closely with God and living into their names.

Tell participants that in this session, they will learn how God gave Abram and Sarai new names, and what those names revealed about God's promises to them.

Opening Prayer

Pray the following prayer, or one of your own choosing:

God of Abraham and Sarah, we know that no matter what is going on in our lives, you will show up! Trusting that you will show up now, in this place, as you have promised, open our hearts to the work of your Spirit as we seek to know and be known more fully. Amen.

Learning Together

Video Study and Discussion

In chapter 3, the author invites us to encounter the God who continues to show up in the lives of Abram and Sarai, gifting them with the new names that reflect the promise fulfilled in them with the birth of a son. After viewing the video segment, discuss some of the following:

- We hear that Abram and Sarai receive new names from God. What are those names, and what do they mean? How do those names reflect how God's promises to them were ultimately fulfilled?
- We remember that the spiritual heritage of Abraham is belief. What does Jacob Armstrong assert is the spiritual heritage of Sarah? Why?
- How do you respond to the idea that nothing is too hard for God? Have you found this to be true in your own life? If so, in what ways?
- Armstrong invites us to embrace the idea that it's okay to laugh with God along the journey. What does he mean? When, if ever, has this been your experience?

Book and Bible Study and Discussion

Explore Further the Story of Abraham and Sarah

Invite participants to imagine themselves to be either Sarah or Abraham. Call their attention to how Jacob Armstrong sets the scene for considering the Scripture, noting that Abraham was sitting in the doorway of the tent in the heat of the day. Sarah was presumably inside the tent.

Ask group members to close their eyes and listen with the ears of either Abraham or Sarah, imagining themselves in the scene. Then read aloud Genesis 18:1-15. Allow for a moment or two of silence. Invite participants who imagined themselves to be Abraham to respond to the following:

- As you sat in the doorway to your tent, were you napping, as Jacob Armstrong suggests?
- If you were not sleeping away the heat of the midday, what were you thinking about? Were you pondering your new name and what it implied? Were you thinking about the gap between what God had promised you and what you could see about your present life?
- When the strangers appeared, who did you think they were? Did you have an inkling that they might represent the presence of the Holy One, or were you merely offering them the hospitality required of you by your culture?
- How did you feel about hearing from God yet one more time that you would be the father of a great nation?

Encourage the "Abrahams" to give additional responses about their thoughts and feelings not addressed in the questions. Now invite those who imagined themselves to be Sarah to respond to some of these questions:

- What were you doing in the tent as your husband was passing time sitting in the doorway? Were you resting inside? Were you engaging in the household tasks of cooking or cleaning?

- What did you think when the three strangers appeared out of the desert? Were you glad to set aside what you were doing to prepare a meal for them? Were you impatient about the extra unexpected work? Or did you feel some other emotion?
- When you heard the stranger's promise of a baby boy, did you have a good, private chuckle, as the author suggests? Or did you throw back your head and laugh out loud, thinking your husband and his guest would be too engrossed in their conversation to notice?
- Did you know it was the Lord who was speaking?
- Why did you deny that you had laughed? Were you afraid of offending the stranger? Or did you simply blurt out a denial? How did you feel when the Lord challenged your denial?
- As an elderly woman, how did you feel about the prospect of having a baby?

Give the "Sarahs" the opportunity to also give additional responses about their thoughts and feelings not addressed in the questions.

Now ask participants to maintain their roles as you read aloud Genesis 21:1-7. After again allowing a few moments of silence, ask:

- How does each of you—Abraham or Sarah—respond to this unlikely and amazing event, the birth of your son?

Examine Radical Hospitality

Armstrong invites us to consider what being a part of this portion of Abraham and Sarah's story implies for us today. Ask someone to describe briefly the imperative for hospitality in the ancient Middle East described by the author. Remind them that shelter is a basic need of all people and that the arid landscape in which Abraham and Sarah lived was a hostile environment where turning persons away might be life-threatening.

Invite someone to read aloud Hebrews 12:3 (also found in the book). Discuss the following:

- What does the author tell us about how we can determine if a stranger on our doorstep is the Holy One?
- In the face of uncertainty about who we may actually be encountering, how are we commanded to treat the stranger?
- What kinds of people does Jesus call us to welcome? In our contemporary context, what sort of people can you identify to whom we may offer hospitality? What are the implications for us as we seek to follow Jesus more faithfully? What specific ministries do you think might constitute throwing an extravagant party for God?

Reflect on Seeing Stars in Midday

Recall for the group a total eclipse experienced by a large number of people living in the United States. Ask volunteers who were in an area where the eclipse was total to describe the experience. Describe what Armstrong's brother told him could happen in a total eclipse, where the sky became so dark that stars emerged.

Ask a volunteer to summarize briefly Jacob Armstrong's story of the program STARS that he remembers from his middle school days, in which students came on stage wearing shirts emblazoned with words such as "heroin" on one side and "hope" on the other. Point out that in the same way that nothing is too hard for God, even making stars visible in midday, we can believe that God is able to turn things around even in the most impossible situations.

Distribute sheets of paper and markers. Invite the group to reflect in silence on what difficult situation or seemingly intractable problem they are presently experiencing in their own lives. It might be something that affects the entire culture, such as climate change or violence, or it could be something deeply personal affecting them as individuals, like a broken relationship or an addiction. On one side of the paper, ask them to print a word that represents that situation or problem. On the other side of the paper, ask them to print a word that represents turning that situation around or transforming that problem. Then encourage participants to reflect on not only how God might turn things around but how they might discern where and how they are being called to act.

More Activities (Optional)

Explore New Testament Passages

The author points us to stories that Jesus told about what makes a good "God party." Form two small groups and assign to one the parable of the lost sheep (Luke 15:1-7) and to the other the parable of the lost coin (Luke 15:8-10). Ask them to read the parable and discuss:

- The author suggests that the parable of the lost sheep might better be named the parable of the crazy shepherd, and perhaps the same might be applied to the parable of the lost coin. Why? Do you agree? Why or why not?
- Why does he suggest that those of us who find ourselves in God's family need to be more prepared to throw parties than we currently are? How do you respond?

Encounter the Implications of Hospitality

Invite the group to prepare for an exercise in the spiritual practice of hospitality. Ask participants to take a few minutes to jot down in their journals the names of people they will encounter in the coming week—family members, friends, acquaintances, and work or school colleagues. In addition to that list, have them jot down others whose names they may not know, but with whom their paths cross on a regular basis—checkout clerks in stores, postal workers, those who routinely travel on the same bus or train, and the like.

After allowing time for participants to work, ask volunteers to assign names to the people in the second category, and jot these down on a large sheet of paper to jog everyone's memory as to persons they may not have thought of.

Call the group's attention to the posted questions. Point out that acting in hospitable ways is not about being best friends with every person with whom you may interact or encounter in the course of a day. But it is about trying to view that person as someone other than a stranger. Choose one or more people from the list, and ask volunteers to name ways to show hospitality—for example, acting with empathy instead of impatience with a store clerk who is short-tempered. Encourage participants to practice hospitality in the coming week, bearing in mind that the stranger at their tent door may be the Holy One.

Wrapping Up

Remind the group that in addition to being prepared to show extravagant hospitality when the Holy One shows up, the author tells us that Abraham and Sarah's story affirms that it's okay to laugh with God along the journey. Invite the group to call out responses to the following, popcorn style:

- I experience joy when I think about God's extravagant promise to _____.
- God's family is so crazy and messed up that I can't help but laugh about _____ .

Remind participants to read chapter 4 before the next session.

Closing Activity

Sing or recite together a song of joy, such as "I've Got Peace Like a River," "I've Got the Joy, Joy, Joy, Joy Down in My Heart," or "You Shall Go Out with Joy."

Closing Prayer

Pray the following, or a prayer of your choosing:

Make us ever more aware, O Holy One, that you may show up in unlikely places as a stranger in disguise. Open our eyes to your presence and our hearts to surprising joy. Amen.

4

LOSS AND PROMISE IN THE FAMILY OF GOD

Planning the Session

Session Goals

As a result of conversations and activities connected with this session, group members should begin to

- explore further, through the story of Abraham and Sarah, what Scripture reveals about God's messy family;
- examine loss in God's family;
- reflect on responding to personal losses.

Scriptural Foundation

Sarah lived to be a hundred and twenty-seven years old. She died at Kiriath Arba (that is, Hebron) in the land of Canaan, and Abraham went to mourn for Sarah and to weep over her.

(Genesis 23:1-2)

Special Preparation

- Have available journaling materials for anyone who did not bring a notebook or an electronic device.
- As Jacob Armstrong observes, some of those in the group are likely experiencing loss in their lives right now—loss of a loved one, of a marriage, of a child living at home, of a job. Be sensitive to how the subject matter of this session may be affecting those for whom loss is immediate and painful.
- For the activity of examining loss in God's family, print each of the following statements on separate large sheets of paper:
  - ◊ Vows do not exempt us from brokenness.
  - ◊ Intimacy does not exempt us from honor.
- Place each sheet on a table, or post the sheets at an interval around your space at a height where participants can reach them for jotting down responses.
- Decide if you will use either of the optional additional activities.
- If you decide to renew baptismal vows, you will need a bowl, water, and perhaps a towel. Alternatively, you may want to have participants reaffirm their commitment to Jesus Christ by repeating the questions and answers your church uses when someone makes a public confession of faith.
- Choose a hymn for the closing activity. "Blest Be the Tie That Binds" is suggested, but you may prefer a hymn commonly sung at a funeral, such as "Great Is Thy Faithfulness" or "For All the Saints," or one that affirms God's presence and comfort such as "Near to the Heart of God" or "When We Are Living." Obtain lyrics and, if needed, arrange for accompaniment.

Getting Started

Opening Activity

Welcome participants as they arrive. Gather together. Ask a volunteer or two about their experiences in the previous week of reflecting, not only about how God might turn difficult or painful situations around, but how they themselves might discern where and how they are being called to act. Ask participants to indicate their response to the following with a show of hands:

- Who has taken solemn vows?

Invite volunteers to name the occasion when vows were called for. If no one mentions vows other than the marriage vows, point out that we make vows and signal our commitment when we join the church, when we are sworn in for elected office, and when we join the armed forces.

Call the group's attention to the story Jacob Armstrong relates at the beginning of chapter 4 about when he presided over the renewal of marriage vows. Note that he assures us that the couple was bound to have experienced many losses, and perhaps even times when those vows were set aside or broken, over the fifty years of their marriage; yet they were willing to renew their vows with a sense of hope.

Ask the group to consider times when they themselves have experienced broken vows or disappointments. Discuss:

- In the face of loss you may have experienced or pain that has come as a result of broken promises, think of how you feel about making new promises. Are you ready to give up, or do you still feel hopeful about new possibilities for promises in your life?

Tell the group that in this session they will delve more deeply into the relationship between loss and promise.

Opening Prayer

Pray the following prayer, or one of your own choosing:

Loving God, we acknowledge that loss is a part of living. Some of us are experiencing the pain of a fresh loss right now, at this very moment. Some of us have known the regret of promises we have failed to keep, of vows broken, of relationships damaged. Make us aware of your presence with us now, as we seek to explore what the story of your family can reveal to us. Amen.

Learning Together

Video Study and Discussion

In chapter 4, we discover that every family, however normal, experiences loss. In relationships, we experience promises broken as well as promises kept. We encounter the paradox that in God's family, brokenness, however painful, can lead to deeper intimacy and the renewal of vows. After viewing the video segment, discuss some of the following:

- Jacob Armstrong observes that while an exploration of Genesis 23 could have been left out, he believes that it is necessary to encounter its truths in order to understand them. Why? Do you agree or disagree?
- He asserts that solemn vows do not exempt us from brokenness and that brokenness can have repercussions for generations. When, if ever, have you experienced such repercussions or observed them in others?
- Armstrong suggests that the more deeply we love, the more we lose. How do you respond?
- What does he mean when he says loss leads to a renewal of vows in God's family? Do you agree? What has been your response to experiences of loss in a relationship?

Book and Bible Study and Discussion

Explore Further the Story of Abraham and Sarah

On a board or a large sheet of paper, print the following:

- Verses 1-2; 3-4; 5-6; 7-8; 10-11; 12-13; 14-15; 16; 17-20.

Tell the group they will read aloud Genesis 23 round-robin style, with each person in turn reading a few verses. Take a moment for participants to identify and read over their assigned verses; then have them read the passage aloud.

Form smaller groups of three persons each. Assign to each person in each smaller group one of the following ideas from the chapter:

- Vows do not exempt us from brokenness.
- Brokenness can lead us to deeper intimacy.
- Intimacy does not exempt us from honor.

Ask each person to review in silence what the text says to explain the idea, as well as any examples the author gives from the story of Abraham. Then ask them to discuss these ideas in their small group, formulating any questions and teasing out key points.

After allowing a few minutes for small groups to discuss, ask each group to report one or more insights they had about vows, as well as any questions or points on which they took issue with what the author observed.

Examine Loss in God's Family

Ask the group to review what the author has to say (in both the chapter and the video segment) about the experience of loss in God's family. Call their attention to the two statements you posted (vows do not exempt us from brokenness; intimacy does not exempt us from honor).

Form two small groups, and assign one of the two statements to each group. Ask participants in each group to read the material in the chapter under the heading "Brokenness." Ask the group considering the statement about vows to also read Genesis 16:1-4, and ask the group considering the statement about intimacy to quickly review Genesis 23. Both small groups should be prepared to summarize their discussion. Come together in the large group to discuss questions or key ideas that came up in the small group discussion.

Call the large group's attention to the other key idea the author puts forth in that section of the chapter: brokenness can lead us to deeper intimacy. Discuss the following:

- Jacob Armstrong acknowledges that in some extreme situations, such as abuse, deeper intimacy may be thwarted. What other situations can you think of that might preclude the deepening of intimacy?
- In any case, are there aspects of accountability that you believe must come into play after vows are broken in order for the affected people to move forward? If so, what elements can you name?
- Recall that in the video segment, Armstrong notes that brokenness can have repercussions for generations. Do you think it is better for people who have experienced brokenness in relationships to keep that fact from other family members? Alternatively, are there some situations in which the truth is necessary, both for healing and for going forward? If so, can you name one such situation?

Reflect on Responding to Personal Losses

We read that honor leads to a deeper experience of love. The author suggests that the closer we become, the more we should honor each other, so that we find a deeper experience of love, both with close friends and family and with God. But paradoxically, the more deeply we love, the more we lose. Discuss:

- Jacob Armstrong notes that in God's family, we can say "I believe" and "I don't understand" in the same breath. How do you respond? Have you ever been in a situation of loss in which those seemingly contradictory statements applied?

Invite participants to reflect for a few minutes on the following and to respond in writing in their journals:

- What losses have I experienced in the past—death of a family member, loss of a job, breaking of marriage vows, betrayal of a close friendship, or other loss? How did I deal with that loss? Did I move away from others and isolate myself, or was I able to move forward and commit more deeply in the face of loss?
- Was my loss the result of vows, either explicitly or implicitly made, being broken by someone close to me? by me?
- How, if at all, have I sought to renew those vows?
- If I am experiencing the pain of a very recent loss, how am I presently dealing with it? Am I able to reach out to God in prayer, even if I have no words? Have I reached out to others in the family of God for comfort? Have they reached out to me?

Encourage group members to continue to reflect on experiences of loss in the coming days.

More Activities (Optional)

Explore John 11

Invite participants to read John 11, the account of the death of Lazarus. Also ask them to read over Armstrong's commentary on the Scripture. Discuss the following:

- The author observes that in times of loss we are called to come closer. Describe how Jesus lived this out in John 11.
- We are told that when Lazarus died, Jesus renewed relationships and promises by bringing life where others saw only death. In your own experiences of the loss of loved ones to death, where we cannot actually restore life to the one we love, how do we bring life to the situation?
- Do you find comfort in the idea that Jesus weeps with us when we experience loss?

Write a Personal Renewal of a Vow

Invite participants to consider where in their own lives they need to renew a vow. This might be an explicit vow such as the marriage vow that has actually been broken through infidelity or perhaps weakened by inattention or indifference. It might be a failure to continue to deepen one's commitment to discipleship. Or it could be a weakening or a dulling of implicit commitments to ethical behavior in the workplace, or drifting away from attentiveness to a friendship.

In their journals, ask participants to write a statement renewing that implicit or explicit vow, using this format or some other that works for them:

> In my commitment to (person or principle), I confess that I have failed in the following ways: _____.
> As a sign of my renewed commitment, I promise to _____.

Though this renewal of a vow is a private one meant primarily for the eyes of the person making it, encourage participants whose renewed commitment is to a relationship to somehow make that person aware of it. If the renewed commitment is to a principle, such as a stronger ethical stance in the workplace, they may want to reread their renewed vow on a regular basis.

Wrapping Up

Armstrong observes that in the family of God, we don't give up on love and God won't give up on us. We go through tough situations, and we renew our vows. Refer the group to the story with which the author closes the chapter—his account of running away from God for the first time at the age of seventeen. Ask someone to tell how Armstrong's youth pastor reached out to him.

He ends the chapter by asking us if today, as the family of God, we want to renew our vows. Tell the group that while there are many personal vows we can seek to renew in order to move forward, Armstrong is referring here to the vows we take when we declare our faith publicly in joining the particular part of the family of God that is our congregation. Since baptism calls us to a life of Christian discipleship, and since we can never fully live up to the vows we take to follow Jesus Christ, one way to signal a recommitment to those vows is to experience a renewal of one's baptism.

If your group chooses to renew the act of baptism, ask the group to form a circle and sit in silence for a moment or two. Then hold the bowl of water out to the person on your right and invite him or her to dip hands in the water. Say these words, or words of your choosing: "[Name], renew your commitment to be a part of God's family. Remember your baptism and be thankful." That person then extends the bowl to the person on his or her right and repeats the words. Continue around the circle until the bowl is returned to you. Close with a time of silence.

Remind participants to read chapter 5 before the next session.

Closing Activity

As a sign of both our connection within the family of God and our reliance on the God of steadfast love, sing or recite together "Blest Be the Tie That Binds."

Closing Prayer

Pray the following, or a prayer of your choosing:

Steadfast God, in the midst of all the difficult situations that life can bring, we affirm that you never give up on us. No matter what loss we experience or how badly it hurts, no matter how often we turn away from others and even from you, we know that your love endures. For that, we give thanks! Amen.

5

PROMISE MAKER
AND PROMISE KEEPER

Planning the Session

Session Goals

As a result of conversations and activities connected with this session, group members should begin to

- explore further, through the stories of Jacob and Joseph, what Scripture reveals about God's messy family;
- examine the significance of dreams in the stories;
- reflect on God's promises passed down to us.

Scriptural Foundation

> *"I am the Lord, the God of your father Abraham and the God of Isaac. I will give you and your descendants the land on which you are lying. Your descendants will be like the dust of the earth, and you will spread*

*out to the west and to the east, to the north and to the
south. All peoples on earth will be blessed through you
and your offspring. I am with you and will watch over
you wherever you go, and I will bring you back to this
land. I will not leave you until I have done what I have
promised you."*

(Genesis 28:13-15)

*Then Jacob made a vow, saying, "If God will be with
me and will watch over me on this journey I am taking
and will give me food to eat and clothes to wear so that
I return safely to my father's household, then the Lord
will be my God."*

(Genesis 28:20-21)

*"Here comes that dreamer!" they said to each other.
"Come now, let's kill him and throw him into one of
these cisterns and say that a ferocious animal devoured
him. Then we'll see what comes of his dreams."*

(Genesis 37:19-20)

Special Preparation

- Provide writing materials for those who did not bring a notebook or an electronic device for journaling.
- On a large sheet of paper or a board, print the following: remarriage; death; conflict or division among family members; in-laws who don't get along with their daughters-in-law.
- Decide if you will use any of the optional additional activities. For creating a reminder, gather available art materials: drawing paper and crayons or markers, at a minimum; but also glue, tissue paper, magazines, and scissors if you so choose.

- Choose a hymn for the closing activity. One possibility is the hymn "Standing on the Promises." Obtain lyrics and, if needed, arrange for accompaniment.

Getting Started

Opening Activity

As participants arrive, welcome them. Remind them of the activity in the previous session in which they renewed a vow that they had taken. Because that vow was a private one meant primarily for their eyes only, encourage them to continue to reflect on that vow and its implications for changed behavior or enhanced relationships.

Ask the group to think about words or phrases that describe the messier aspects of their own family life—perhaps words like conflict with teenagers, divorce, difficult relationships with stepchildren or ex-spouses, and the like. Reassure the group that this list is for their eyes only, with no obligation for them to share with anyone else.

Gather together. Invite volunteers to call out, popcorn style, descriptors (not necessarily on their personal lists) that they imagine might make family life messy. Call the group's attention to the list of words and phrases you posted, and ask:

- What do these words and phrases have in common? How are they different from each other?

If no one responds, refer the group to chapter 5 and point out that these are words the author uses to describe the more problematic aspects of Abraham's growing family legacy. Yet, as he points out, these situations could be (and perhaps are) on the lists of people in the group. In this session, they will engage in a deeper exploration of Abraham's legacy as it played out in the lives of his descendants and what that has to tell us about God's steadfast promises.

Opening Prayer

Pray the following prayer, or one of your own choosing:

Promise Keeper God, we affirm that while we fall short of keeping our promises over and over again, you never do. As we explore the scriptural story of your family, remind us again of your enduring promises that never fail. Amen.

Learning Together

Video Study and Discussion

In chapter 5, we encounter the truth that we are part of a family of promise makers, promise keepers, and promise breakers. Yet our God of promises will be faithful to the promises even when we are not. We discover that the promise God extended to Abraham and Sarah is the same promise passed down to Jacob and Joseph. After viewing the video segment, discuss some of the following:

- Jacob Armstrong calls our attention to another network TV series about family, this time about *Seinfeld*, a "family" of four single adults living in New York City. He focuses on an episode in which Jerry reserves a car through a car rental agency. In Jerry's view, what is the important part about taking a reservation? What does this have to say about promises?
- What is the significance of dreams in Jacob's story? How do you view your own dreams? What significant role, if any, do dreams play in your life?
- Armstrong notes that no matter what has come before in our family heritage, we are not bound by our family's past. Why? In his view, how is the curse of a sketchy past broken?
- What is the significance of the number 129 for Armstrong and his wife? Can you name any significant symbols or signs that play a similar role in your own life?

Book and Bible Study and Discussion

Explore the Stories of Jacob and Joseph

Remind the group that in the previous session, following Sarah's death, the story of Abraham and Sarah concluded with the marriage of Isaac and Rebekah. Invite participants to quickly scan chapter 5 under the heading "Abraham's Growing Legacy." Together, construct a time line of the significant events the author names in the continuing story of Abraham and Sarah's descendants. As participants call out responses, jot down in order the events between the marriage of Isaac and Rebekah and the story of what is commonly referred to as Jacob's ladder.

Invite one or more volunteers to read aloud Genesis 28:10-22. Discuss:

- What happened when Jacob attempted to run away from the promise that he must have heard about his entire life? Have you ever had the experience of attempting to run away from God? If so, what can you tell about it?
- What was the significance of stones in Abraham's story? in the story of Jacob's dream?
- How was Jacob transformed by the vow he took? Do you think God's promises have the power to transform the lives of people, even those who rely on tricks and lies as Jacob did? Why or why not?

Use the same process to work further in constructing a time line of Joseph's story, asking participants to scan the material under the heading "God Passes Down Dreams" and then jotting down events listed there from Joseph's life.

Continue the story by having one or more volunteers read aloud Genesis 37:12-28.

- What was the impact of Joseph's dream on his brothers? What emotions on the part of both Joseph and his brothers does

the author suggest might have led to the brothers' aggression
against their sibling?

- What effect did all this have, not on the dreams Joseph
reported having but on his larger dreams for his future?
How do you think the brothers' actions might have affected
those dreams?

- In your own life, have there been times when your actions
have negatively affected your hopes and dreams for the future?
If so, can you describe what happened?

Examine the Significance of Dreams

Form two smaller groups. Assign to one group the story of Jacob
and his dream, and to the other group the story of Joseph and his
dreams as recorded in Genesis 37. Give each group a large sheet of
paper, and ask groups to discuss and then answer the following about
the dreams of their assigned character:

- Describe your character. Based on what you read in Scripture,
what kind of a person was he?

- Describe the setting of your character's dream(s). Where and
when did the dream(s) take place?

- Tell about the content of your character's dream(s). How did
he interpret or describe the dream? What, if anything, did he
do in response to the dream(s)?

Allow a few minutes for groups to work; then ask each one to
report to the large group. Discuss some of the following in the large
group:

- Where, if at all, do you see any similarities between the
characters and temperaments of Jacob and Joseph?

- Based on their characters as revealed in these stories, would
you have expected either man to carry God's promise forward?
Why or why not?

- What contrasts do you see between the dreams of the two men? In what ways does each dream have to do with greatness?

The story of Joseph teaches us that life usually turns out differently than the way we dreamed it would.

- Jacob Armstrong suggests that instead of this being a negative, it can be one of the great positives of being on the adventure with God. How do you respond?
- He observes that we may dream, but we often don't perceive what the fulfillment of our dreams may look like; therefore we must constantly adjust our expectations regarding timing and promises. If you agree, can you cite an example from your own life that backs this up? If not, how do you view this reality of life?
- Regardless of whether our expectations are unmet, met, or exceeded, how are we called to live?

Reflect on God's Promises

Remind the group that one identifying characteristic of the church is that everyone is invited to dream—that is, God's family dreams. Armstrong points out that the promise God made to Abraham and Sarah was the same promise that came to Jacob in a dream and would later be the same promise made to Joseph. And, says Armstrong, God is making that same promise to all of us: that we will experience greatness, blessing, and the ability to pass those things down.

Invite participants to reflect on the following and then to respond in writing in their journals:

- In what ways have I been a promise maker? a promise keeper? a promise breaker?
- What dreams do I have for being a part of God's loving purpose for the world?
- In what ways are my dreams for my life being met? How have dreams I have cherished been unmet up to this point in my

life? If unmet, how could I adjust my expectations so that I can continue to live faithfully and with integrity?

- Am I able to identify ways my dreams have been exceeded? If so, how am I expressing my gratitude to God?

Encourage participants to continue reflecting in the coming week on dreams they may have had for their lives—met, unmet, or exceeded. Suggest that they also pay attention to the dreams they have while sleeping.

More Activities (Optional)

Explore Scripture

Form pairs or small groups, depending on the size of your group, to explore more deeply the stories of Jacob's early life. Assign one of the following to each pair or small group: Genesis 25:19-28; 25:29-34; 27:1-29; 27:30-40; 27:41-45; 28:6-9. Ask each group to read the assigned account. Afterward, in the large group, ask each pair or small group to summarize their portion of the story. Encourage participants to read Genesis 29–33 on their own to become familiar with the rest of Jacob's story.

Create a Reminder of God's Presence and Promises

Remind participants that in both the video segment and in the book chapter, they learned about the significance of the number 129 for Jacob and Rachel Armstrong. Invite them to take a moment to consider if there is a symbol or sign that could serve as a reminder of God's promises and presence in their lives. It might be a number, such as the citation for a Bible verse that is significant to them, just as Genesis 29 is significant for the Armstrongs. Or it might be poetry or a hymn lyric.

After allowing some time for group members to identify such a sign or symbol for themselves, invite them to create a tangible reminder. Distribute sheets of drawing paper and colored markers or crayons, as well as any other art materials you have available, and invite them to create a reminder that they can post on a refrigerator, a bathroom mirror, over a desk, or anyplace where they will see it daily. Some may want to take a digital photo of the reminder and use it as a screen saver for a pad or computer.

Wrapping Up

If your group did the optional activity "Create a Reminder of God's Presence and Promises," ask group members to share the signs or symbols, along with the tangible reminders they made, if they feel comfortable doing so.

If your group did not do the optional activity, remind them that in both the video segment and in the book chapter, they learned about the significance of the number 129 for Jacob and Rachel Armstrong. Invite them to take a moment to consider if there is a symbol or sign that could serve as a reminder of God's promises and presence in their lives. It might be a number, such as the citation for a Bible verse that is significant to them, just as Genesis 29 is significant for the Armstrongs. Or it might be poetry or a hymn lyric. When they have identified their reminder, encourage them to find ways to think about it on a regular basis.

Remind participants to read chapter 6 before the next session.

Closing Activity

In the opening of the chapter, Jacob Armstrong relates the story of baptizing six-year-old Jake. Armstrong tells us that baptism is an expression of our heritage. Though we may not completely understand the promises we make at that time, and though we will inevitably fail to fully keep them, we make promises anyway. And, as the group may have experienced in the renewal of baptism in the last session, we can renew our promises even as we remember God's promises to us.

Sing or recite together "Standing on the Promises" or another hymn of your choice.

Closing Prayer

Pray the following, or a prayer of your choosing:

Covenant God, we give thanks that you are trustworthy and that your promises are sure—even though we are much less trustworthy than you are. By your Spirit, make us ever more aware of your enduring presence with us, even as we fail. Amen.

6

THE BEAUTY
OF IMPERFECTION

Planning the Session

Session Goals

As a result of conversations and activities connected with this session, group members should begin to:

- explore further, through the story of Joseph, what Scripture reveals about God's messy family;
- examine lessons about what to expect in God's family;
- reflect on ourselves as people of promise.

Scriptural Foundation

> *"You intended to harm me, but God intended it for good to accomplish what is now being done, the saving of many lives."*
>
> *(Genesis 50:20)*

Special Preparation

- Have available writing materials for anyone who did not bring a notebook or an electronic device for journaling.
- On a large sheet of paper or a board, print the following for the opening activity: Something in my life that I did not expect to happen was _____.
- For the activity of examining what we can expect, print each of the following on a separate large sheet of paper, and then post the sheets of paper at intervals around your space or on tabletops and provide felt-tipped markers.
  - ◊ Expect many tears.
  - ◊ Expect so much forgiveness.
  - ◊ God can take what others mean for harm and use it to save lives.
  - ◊ You never know what God may be up to!
- Decide if you will use either of the optional additional activities. If you explore Scripture more deeply, each participant will need access to a Bible.
- For the closing activity, print the litany response on a large sheet of paper or a board and post it where it can easily be seen.

Getting Started

Opening Activity

Welcome participants to this final session of the study. Call their attention to the open-ended prompt you posted, and ask them to jot down a response. When most have arrived and have had a chance to respond, gather together. Invite volunteers who are willing to do so to report on any insights they may have had about dreams for which their expectations were met or exceeded.

Look together at the responses made to the prompt, and invite a volunteer or two to elaborate on how they responded. Ask:

- How, if at all, did this unexpected occurrence cause you to change your expectations?
- Did the occurrence throw you for a loop or disorient you? Or did you view this unexpected event as an opportunity to adjust your expectations of life, so you could continue to live faithfully and with integrity? What adjustments did you make?

Tell the group that as they continue to explore Joseph's story, they will delve more deeply into how a person's life can change in an instant, permanently altering the trajectory of a life.

Opening Prayer

Pray the following prayer, or one of your own choosing:

Make us aware of your presence with us, O Holy One, as we seek to hear you speaking through the stories of your family that we find in Scripture. In the face of the unexpected, surprise us with fresh insights. Amen.

Learning Together

Video Study and Discussion

In the final chapter of the study, we look closely at episodes in Joseph's eventful life, discovering that we all have similar experiences in our messy relationships with others. We examine Joseph's experiences of betrayal and bondage, of being blindsided, and of being abandoned. Paradoxically, we also encounter in Joseph's story the affirmation that nothing will take us away from the reach and presence of God. After viewing the video segment, discuss some of the following:

- Describe how Joseph was betrayed, and by whom. Respond to the question posed by the author: Which betrayal do you think of as you try to fall asleep?
- Jacob Armstrong notes that while most of us have never been subjected to the kind of bondage Joseph experienced, we may

know how it feels to be weighed down and chained up.
What has you weighed down and chained up?
- Have you ever been blindsided by events or by a relationship, as Joseph was? If so, did the experience leave a mark, as Armstrong suggests? As a result of any of these experiences, were you left feeling abandoned by the people you trusted? by God?
- Armstrong invites us to attend to the phrase "But God . . ." To what truth is he pointing?

Book and Bible Study and Discussion

Explore Further the Story of Joseph

Refresh the group's memory about Joseph's story by reading aloud the first three paragraphs of chapter 6, which recount the story of Joseph being sold into slavery. Tell the group that because the story of Joseph encompasses a number of chapters of Scripture, Jacob Armstrong provides us with a brief summary and salient points about relevant parts of the narrative.

Form three small groups. Assign one of the following accounts to each group: Joseph and Potiphar's wife; Joseph in prison; Joseph serving as second-in-command to Pharaoh, saving Egypt from famine, and again encountering his brothers. Each group should quickly scan the material in the chapter in search of answers to the following questions. (Note that every episode may not show evidence of all four elements— betrayal, bondage, blindsiding, and abandonment.)

- In this account, where do you see evidence of Joseph being betrayed?
- Where do you find evidence of his being in bondage?
- In what ways is he blindsided?
- In what circumstances is he abandoned—and to what?

Back in the large group, ask each small group to summarize their findings. Then discuss the following:

- Imagine being Joseph and experiencing the events and situations we have just explored. In what ways do you think Joseph had to adjust his expectations?
- We read that Joseph dreamed about himself and interpreted the dreams of others. What dreams do you imagine he had for his life?
- Is there evidence in these accounts that God abandoned Joseph? If so, what is it? Conversely, do you see evidence that God was with Joseph? Where?

Examine Lessons About What to Expect

Armstrong invites us to consider the following: What do we learn from Joseph that we can expect in God's messy family? Call the group's attention to the sheets you posted before the session, each with one of the lessons that Armstrong identifies. Ask participants to take a few moments to read over the statements and to review what the author says about each one. Then ask them to go from sheet to sheet, adding comments and observations about any of the lessons, as well as questions they may have.

After allowing a few minutes for participants to respond to the lessons, gather together again, and invite volunteers to expand on one or more of their comments. If the following do not surface in the discussion, discuss them now:

- The author notes that even as beautiful things were happening, Joseph carried the grief of the prison floor and the betrayal of the pit. What do you think he means? How do you respond?
- Jacob Armstrong suggests that if we don't forgive, we stay chained up. Do you agree? Is there ever a situation in which forgiveness must be withheld? If so, can you name the circumstances?
- He notes that Joseph's story doesn't teach us that God makes bad things so good can come out of it. What do you think he means? Do you agree?

Reflect on Ourselves as People of Promise

Armstrong observes that God's family must claim this statement: "But God . . ." Invite volunteers to explain what he means and to give examples from Joseph's life.

Armstrong then poses these questions:

- What is your story?
- What do you look at and think: Why did this happen in my life?
- What can God do?

Ask participants to think about these questions and consider where in their lives they have experienced situations or events that were unexpected, that altered the way they expected their life to go. Ask them to take a few minutes to list one or more of these events in their journal. After each situation or event, ask them to write down the words, "But God . . ." and to reflect on what, in retrospect, God did in their lives to redeem the situation.

In some situations, it may be that a person cannot yet discern God working at all. In that case, invite them to reflect on what God might do or could do in the future to work for good. Ask them in the coming days to pray for discernment about what God might do in and through their lives, messy though they may be.

More Activities (Optional)

Explore Scripture

Assign one of the following passages to each person to read (or to pairs in a large group): Genesis 39; 40; 41:1-36; 41:37-57; 42:1-25; 42:26-34; 43; 44:1-17; 44:18-34; 45. Back in the large group, ask each individual or pair to summarize their portion of the story.

Get in Character

Armstrong invites us to consider various characters in the story of Joseph and how they might have been thinking that Joseph was a special person in some way. Invite participants to choose one of the following characters: Potiphar, Potiphar's wife, the prison warden, Pharaoh. Invite each person to write a brief reflection from the perspective of their chosen character, beginning with the sentence, "There's something about this guy."

When everyone has had time to reflect and write their responses, invite volunteers to read what they wrote, ideally with one volunteer at least for each of the characters. Discuss:

- The author writes that everywhere Joseph went, he was thrown into pits. What does he mean?
- What special qualities did each of the characters seem to identify in Joseph?
- In the beginning of Joseph's story, what qualities of Joseph—good and bad—do you think his brothers would have named? What qualities might they have named at the end of the story?
- Among the characters who recognized Joseph's special qualities, who acted on that knowledge to Joseph's benefit? Who acted to hurt him?

Wrapping Up

On a large sheet of paper or a board, print the words "God's Messy Family" and invite participants to consider the very human characters who were the focus of this study. Remind them that some primary family members who would appear on a family tree—such as Isaac, Rebekah, Rachel, Ishmael, Jacob's second wife Leah, and Jacob's other sons—did not play a central role in this study. If time had allowed a closer study of these people's lives, the group would no doubt have discovered that each of them also exhibited human failings and foibles.

Tell the group that as you name a character, they are to call out words or phrases that exemplify both the positive and negative aspects of that person's character. Jot down each description, and then move on to the next character.

Remind the group that for us, as for Abraham and Sarah's family, God works in and through our lives, as messy as they may be. Through us, despite our failings, God intends to save many things and many people we thought were lost.

Closing Activity

Armstrong observes that the story of Abraham is our story too. What God promises to Abraham and Sarah, God extends to us as well. Invite the group to join in the following closing litany by responding with the posted lines:

Leader: Like Abraham and Sarah, we sometimes feel we are journeying to an unknown land. Our lives can seem empty, directionless, without the hope of new life.

All: **But God says, I will make you a great nation, I will bless you, and I will make your name great. And you will be a blessing.**

Leader: Like Jacob, we may sometimes seek to get our own way through deceit. We may deny those we love some of the things that are rightfully theirs. We may flee relationships that have soured because of our own actions.

All: **But God says, I will make you a great nation, I will bless you, and I will make your name great. And you will be a blessing.**

Leader: Like Joseph, our lives don't usually turn out the way we planned. Sometimes we are weighed down by unmet expectations, chained to old patterns of living, blindsided by events we never saw coming.

All: **But God says, I will make you a great nation, I will bless you, and I will make your name great. And you will be a blessing. Amen.**

Closing Prayer

Pray the following, or a prayer of your choosing:

God whose promises are steadfast and sure, we give thanks that we can embrace our calling as people of promise. By your Spirit, guide us as we seek to be a blessing to the world you love. Amen.

CPSIA information can be obtained
at www.ICGtesting.com
Printed in the USA
LVHW03s0713010718
582339LV00003B/3/P

9 781501 843587